THE
LORD'S SUPPER

THE CELEBRATION OF THE NEW COVENANT

THE
LORD'S
SUPPER

THE CELEBRATION OF THE NEW COVENANT

(An Exerpt from *The New Covenant,*
Published by BenchPress Publishing 2013)

✦BOB EMERY✦

Unless otherwise noted, all Scripture quotations in this book are taken from the New American Standard Bible, © Copyright The Lockman Foundation 1960, 1962, 1963, 1968, 1971, 1972, 1973, 1975, 1977. Used by permission.

Cover Design: Sarah O'Neal
Eve Custom Artwork
se_oneal@yahoo.com
Cover Photo of Bread and Wine courtesy of Kevin Rawlings

Published by:
BenchPress Publishing
P.O. Box 5846
Charlottesville, VA 22905
Website: www.BobEmeryBooks.com

ISBN: 978-0-9669747-6-8
Printed in the USA
ISBN eBook: 978-0-966974-7-4

TABLE OF CONTENTS

THE LORD'S SUPPER

THE CELEBRATION OF THE NEW COVENANT

When people think of the New Testament, they typically think of the collection of writings consisting of the four gospels, the book of Acts, the various epistles written to churches and Christian workers, and then the finale—the book of Revelation. This body of writings, combined with the Old Testament to total sixty-six books, makes up the entire Bible.

However, the New Testament is more than a collection of books and letters glued and stitched together between a leather jacket along with the writings of the Old Testament. The words *testament* and *covenant* are interchangeable. Therefore, to properly think of the New Testament (or the New Covenant), we should understand it as the present, eternal, relational reality between God and his people.

To amplify this point, the word *testament* can also be thought of as a will. When a person's last will and testament is executed after that person has died, the covenant or contract takes effect, and the inheritance is received by those named in the will. As the author of the book of Hebrews wrote:

"For where a covenant is, there must of necessity be the death of the one who made it. For a covenant is valid only when men are dead, for it is never in force while the one who made it lives."

In ancient times, the shedding of blood ratified covenants. The agreement between two parties was made, and then an animal was slain, signifying that if either party failed to meet its obligations in the contract, a similar vengeance or retribution as in the slaying of that animal should be taken out upon them.

With the death of Christ, we received our inheritance as spelled out in the New Covenant. To celebrate that covenant, our Lord initiated for us the Lord's Supper.

Since its inauguration, believers throughout the centuries have participated in celebrating the Lord's Supper. For some, it has been just that—a celebration. But this has not been the case for the vast majority of those who have lifted the cup to their lips and shared in the breaking of the bread over the past two millenniums. For most, it has become an event not marked by joy, but rather by something less satisfying, less fulfilling, and not in keeping with the teaching of the New Covenant. The Lord's Supper as it is most commonly practiced today has become a solemn, superstitious, fearful event that causes the Lord's people to engage in morbid, soul-searching introspection rather than to look joyfully and thankfully into the face of the glorious one who, for the joy before him, paid such a price on their behalf.

Sadly, for most of the believing community, the true meaning of the Lord's Supper has been virtually lost, and its practice has become so misconfigured so as to render it unrecognizable in comparison to the way in which it was practiced in the first century. Draping it in layers of institutionalism, superstition, and religious attitudes borrowed from pagan religion, the enemy has done a magnificent job of robbing the Christian church of our true inheritance in understanding and celebrating the elevated, sacred, and mysterious significance of this simple transaction that governs our relationship with our Creator and Redeemer.

In framing the significance and meaning of Lord's Supper, it is important that we look at it within the overarching theme of the whole Bible. We must ask ourselves, what does this simple but profound sacrament mean in light of God's plan for all eternity, and how does it relate to the New Covenant—the present, eternal, relational reality that governs our relationship with the Father and with his Son, the Lord Jesus Christ?

THE BIBLE IS A LOVE STORY

When we step back from the Scriptures and look at the Bible in its entirety, a simple conclusion emerges. The Bible is a love story. Its bridal theme is central—the love of Christ for his bride.

Take, for example, the stories of these Bible couples:

- Adam and Eve
- Isaac and Rebekah
- Boaz and Ruth
- Esther and the King

- Hosea and Gomer
- Solomon and the Shulamite
- God and Israel (even in the Old Testament, Israel is referred to as God's bride)

"Bridal Theology" is a term sometimes used to describe looking at the Scriptures through the lens of its romantic theme.

Down through the ages, there have been believers (considered by some to be Christian mystics) who have tapped into this revelation of God and written about it—people like:

- Origen of Alexandria—third century
- Saint Ambrose and Saint Gregory of Nyssa—fourth century
- Bernard of Clairvaux and William of Saint Thierry—twelfth century
- Saint Teresa of Avila and Saint John of the Cross—sixteenth century
- Madame Guyon—sixteenth–seventeenth century

And many times it resulted in persecution.

If the theme of the Bible is indeed a romance, and if Christ is our Bridegroom and we are his bride, then the Lord's Supper must somehow fit into this theme.

THE LORD'S SUPPER: A WEDDING CELEBRATION

In celebrating the Lord's Supper, we are celebrating our union with our Bridegroom, the King of all kings and Lover of our souls.

From eternity past, long before the world was created, before time, matter, or anything physical had ever been created, God had a plan. It was his purpose—his eternal purpose. That purpose was to have a bride for his Son.

The Father loved his Son so much that he wanted to give him a gift: a bride whom he could love, and who would love him in return, who would be his life companion and rule and reign with him for all eternity.

We see the picture, or foreshadowing of that purpose in Genesis chapters 1 and 2, where God created Adam, then put him to sleep. He took a rib from his side to fashion (build) Eve, and the two became one flesh, husband and wife.

With the passage of thousands of years, and when the fullness of time had come, we see the reality of that picture finally fulfilled. Christ came to earth, died on the tree (slept for three days), then rose again. By his Spirit, he has been fashioning (building) his church ever since.

In Revelation 21 and 22, we see God's plan complete: a new heaven and a new earth with the bride (the church—the New Jerusalem) descending out of heaven to become eternally one with Christ (her Bridegroom).

CHRIST AS THE BRIDEGROOM IN THE GOSPELS

Even in the gospels, if we have eyes to see, we can see Christ coming as the Bridegroom. John the Baptizer identified him as such when he said, "He who has the bride is the bridegroom, but the friend of the bridegroom, who stands and hears him, rejoices greatly because of the bridegroom's voice. So this joy of mine has been made full." (John 3:29)

When Christ came out of the water at his baptism, a voice from heaven proclaimed, "This is my beloved Son, in whom I am well-pleased." (Matthew 3:17) A more accurate rendering is found in *Young's Literal Translation of the Bible,* which reads, "This is my Son—the Beloved, in whom I did delight," calling attention to Christ being the fulfillment of King Solomon in the Song of Songs, who was referred to as "The Beloved." In this love song portraying the king and his Shulamite bride, the king pictures Christ, and the Shulamite the church.

In John 4, in the story of the Samaritan woman, we see Christ as the fulfillment of Jacob, who came seeking his bride and found her at the well (Genesis 29, John 4:5–39). The woman in John 4 was a Samaritan—a half-breed, half-Jew, half-Gentile—another picture of the bride that Christ purchased with his own blood.

We see a hint of Christ as the Bridegroom in the first miracle he performed at the wedding in Cana of Galilee in John 2, verses 1–11. When the wine ran out, Jesus's mother said to him, "They have no wine," to which Jesus replied, "Woman, what does that have to do with us? My hour has not yet come." What hour was he referring to? The hour of his wedding! The hour of his wedding had not yet come.

In the passage in Luke in which the Lord initiates the Lord's Supper with his disciples, it says, *"When the hour had come,* he reclined at the table and the apostles with him . . . and when he had taken a cup [of wine] and given thanks, he said, 'Take this and share it among yourselves.'" (Luke 22:14-17)

When our Lord took the Lord's Supper with his disciples, the hour of his wedding had finally come!

ANCIENT JEWISH WEDDING CUSTOMS

We can better begin to understand the significance of the Lord's Supper when we take into account ancient Jewish wedding customs that were observed at the time of Christ. Let's start with the engagement.

In Jewish culture, when a young man and woman became engaged, it was customary for the bridegroom's father to choose the bride for his son. A meeting took place under the supervision of the father of the groom and the father of the bride, and a meal was prepared.

THE NEW COVENANT IS A WEDDING COVENANT

We can see the apostle Paul's spiritual understanding of this concept and of this relationship of Christ as our Bridegroom and God the Father choosing a bride for his Son. We can almost imagine him taking the place of the father of the bride when he wrote to the Corinthians, "For I am jealous for you with a godly jealousy; for I betrothed you to one husband, so that to Christ I might present you as a pure virgin." (2 Corinthians 11:2)

Following the meal, the bridegroom proposed marriage by offering a written contract to the woman called the *ketuba*. This was a legally binding document spelling out in detail the promises and obligations the bridegroom would perform for his bride.

The bride, on the other hand, was not obligated to make *any* promises to her husband. But she had the right of refusal.

The legally binding contract the Lord Jesus offered at the Lord's Supper was the New Covenant. Comparing that to the woman's right of refusal, we see the role of free will in our entrance into this marriage covenant.

"And in the same way the cup, after they had eaten, saying 'This cup which is poured out for you is the new covenant in my blood.'" (1 Corinthians 11:25)

Unlike the Old Covenant, which had conditions ("I will bless you *if* you do this," or "I will curse you *if* you do that") the New Covenant is a *unilateral covenant*. It is one-sided. It consists only of "I wills."

Jeremiah 31:31–34 spells out the terms of the New Covenant.

"'Behold, the days are coming,' declares the Lord, 'when I will make a new covenant with the house of Israel and the house of Judah.'"

- "I will put my law within them and on their heart I will write it."
- "I will be their God, and they shall be my people."
- "I will forgive their iniquity, and their sin I will remember no more."

Once the disciples partook of the cup, in the eyes of God, they had accepted the Bridegroom's proposal. They were legally wed to

Christ! When we partake of the cup of wine, we are proclaiming that Christ is our Bridegroom and we are the bride of Christ. We are his body. We are inseparably one with him. By drinking, the contract has been ratified, and we are legally, once and for all, forever his.

In addition to the contract, the bridegroom offered a price that he was willing to pay for his bride.

Adam gave up bone in order to have his bride. Christ paid the highest price of all. He gave his very life.

"Unless a grain of wheat falls into the earth and dies, it remains alone; but if it dies, it bears much fruit." (John 12:24)

After offering the bride the ketuba (the contract) and declaring the price, the bridegroom would pour wine into a cup. He would drink half and then offer the cup to his prospective bride. If she refused to drink, there would be no wedding. But if she did take the cup and drink, this instantly sealed the marriage! From the moment the wine touched her lips, she became a legally married woman (even though the wedding had not yet been consummated).

The groom would then present the bride with a gift as a tangible reminder that it would not be long before their wedding day and the consummation of their marriage would come. Jesus has given us his Holy Spirit, the reminder that we are betrothed to Christ and that when we finally see him face to face, the complete oneness and marriage relationship that we are longing for will come (Ephesians 1:13–14).

Once the marriage was agreed upon, the bridegroom would go away to prepare a home for them to live in. Usually, he would go to his father's home and "add on" by preparing a place for him and his bride to live. Jesus said, "In my Father's house are many dwelling places; if it were not so, I would have told you, for I go to prepare a place for you. If I go and prepare a place for you, I will come again and receive you to myself; that where I am, there you may be also." (John 14:2-3)

Before parting, the bridegroom made a promise to the bride that he would not drink of the fruit of the vine again until he had finished building their home. Following the Last Supper, Jesus said, "I will not drink of the fruit of the vine from now on until the kingdom of God comes." (Luke 22:18)

The bride, on the other hand, would then spend her time preparing to be the bridegroom's wife.

"'Let us rejoice and be glad and give the glory to him, for the marriage of the Lamb has come and his bride has made herself ready.' It was given to her to clothe herself in fine linen, bright and clean; for the fine linen is the righteous acts of the saints. Then he [the angel] said to me, 'Write, Blessed are those who are invited to the marriage supper of the Lamb.'" (Revelation 19:7-9)

So in the context of the wedding (the wedding supper), the tradition of celebrating with wine not only brought joy to the festivity, but also commemorated that the promise that the complete union between the couple was soon to be fulfilled.

When the bride has made herself ready, Christ, our Bridegroom, will come for his bride. There will be great feasting, and the marriage will be consummated. We will live together—forever in union with him—as husband and wife. This is the consummation when Christ will be All and in all.

So the cup represents a marriage covenant—signifying that we have been married to Christ and are partakers of the New Covenant—of the "I wills" of God.

THE LIFE IS IN THE BLOOD

"Is not the cup of blessing which we bless a sharing in the blood of Christ?" (1 Corinthians 10:16)

The Bible teaches, "the life of all flesh is in the blood." (Leviticus 17:11) To share in the blood of Christ is to share in the Life of Christ. In order for Christ to have a bride, he needed to have a partner who shared the same *Life* that he lived by. On earth, Christ lived by the divine, uncreated Life that he had shared with his Father for all eternity, before the world was ever created. When he rose from the dead and breathed his Spirit into his disciples, it was that *Life* that he breathed into them.

When we take the cup, we celebrate our marriage, our oneness with him. It is our testimony that we have been given the same divine, uncreated, eternal Life that our Bridegroom in heaven lives by. It is a celebration that we, as sons of men, can live by a higher Life—by the very Life of the eternal God! Jesus said, "I came that you might have *life* [Greek: *zoe,* meaning *divine life]* and have it in abundantly!" (John 10:10)

THE BREAD

"For I received from the Lord that which I also delivered to you, that the Lord Jesus in the night in which He was betrayed took bread; and when he had given thanks, He broke it and said, 'This is My body which is given for you; do this in remembrance of Me.'" (1 Corinthians 11:23-24)

In Genesis, the man said, "This is now bone of my bones, and flesh of my flesh. She shall be called Woman, because she was taken out of Man. For this reason a man shall leave his father and his mother, and be joined to his wife [give his body and soul to his wife], and they shall become one flesh." (Genesis 2: 23-24)

Just like Adam became "one flesh" with Eve, Christ became "one spirit" with his bride.

"But the one who joins himself to the Lord is one spirit with him." (1 Corinthians 6:17)

Christ's giving us the bread represents his giving us his body and becoming one with us. By sharing in the bread, we are testifying that we not only have his life living in us and belong to him, but that we all, together, share that same life and belong to one another. By partaking of the bread, we are affirming and celebrating our oneness and eternal union with Christ and with one another. By partaking of the cup, we affirm, are reminded of, and celebrate our wedding vows with the Lord, as spelled out in the New Covenant.

Each time we partake of the wine and the bread, we are also reminded of the simple but eternal principle found in God himself: Without the crushing of the grapes, there could be no wine. Without the dying of the wheat, there could be no bread.

In order for us to receive the life of God and become the bride of Christ, Christ needed to die.

OLD TESTAMENT PICTURES FORESHADOWING THE LORD'S SUPPER: MELCHIZEDEK

"And Melchizedek, king of Salem, brought out bread and wine [to Abraham]; now he was a priest of God Most High. He blessed him and said, 'Blessed be Abram of God Most High, possessor of heaven and earth; and blessed be God Most High, who has delivered your enemies into your hand.' He [Abraham] gave him a tenth of all." (Genesis 14:18-20)

"You [Christ] are a priest forever according to the order of Melchizedek." (Hebrews 7:17)

Melchizedek did not exist before Jesus; Jesus existed before Melchizedek ("Before Abraham was born, *I am*"). Melchizedek's name meant "King of Righteousness." He was also king of Salem, which is "King of Peace" (see Hebrews 7:2).

This Old Testament picture tells us that Christ, our heavenly Bridegroom, who is our righteousness and peace, would come to the people of faith (represented by Abraham, the father of faith), offering them bread and wine, the symbols of the New Covenant.

THE ELEMENTS WITHIN THE HOLY PLACE

In the Holy Place in the tabernacle in the wilderness was the table with the bread of the presence (twelve loaves, one for each of the twelve tribes of Israel) and wine. We are told in Exodus that on that table were the holy dishes, along with pans, jars, and bowls with which to pour drink offerings. These articles were made of pure gold (see Exodus 25:29–30). The drink offering consisted of strong wine (see Exodus 29:38–41, Numbers 28:7). The wine was to be pure in the sense that it was not to be watered down. It was to be potent and of full strength.

Besides the bread and the wine on the table, there was also frankincense.

"Then you shall take fine four and bake twelve cakes with it; two-tenths of an ephah shall be in each cake. You shall set them in two rows, six to a row, on the pure gold table before the Lord. You shall put pure frankincense on each row that it may be a memorial portion for the bread, even an offering by fire to the Lord."

Frankincense was one of the ingredients in the exclusive formula for incense to be burned before the Lord as a sweet-smelling aroma. These substances—the bread, wine, and frankincense— were only available to the priests. There in the Holy Place was where the priests could enjoy intimate communion and fellowship with God. This picture should remind us that it is only as we take up our place as ministering priests to the Lord that we enjoy the intimacy of communion and fellowship with him, as represented by the bread and the wine.

The frankincense (representing resurrection, a sweet-smelling fragrance rising to God) adds to the mystery of this picture. It was not until the resurrection of Christ that we could truly celebrate, with joy, his life and our oneness with him.

THE OLD TESTAMENT TABERNACLE:
ONLY A PICTURE

The tabernacle that Moses constructed in the wilderness was only a pattern or replica of something (someone!) that God revealed to him in the heavens. The writer of Hebrews, when speaking of the priests, said that they served a "copy or a shadow of heavenly things, just as Moses was warned by God when he was about to erect the tabernacle: for, 'See,' he says, 'that you make all things according to the pattern which was shown you on the mountain.'"

Christ is the reality—the "pattern" after which the Old Testament tabernacle was made!

"And the Word became flesh and dwelt [tabernacled] among us, and we saw his glory, glory as of the only begotten from the Father, full of grace and truth."

"And I heard a loud voice from the throne, saying, 'Behold, the tabernacle of God [Christ] is among men.'"

In Christ there has always been the eternal reality of the New Covenant as represented by the wine and the bread pictured in the Holy Place in the tabernacle in the wilderness: *The "I wills" of God and the Life of God are in him, and through him, made available to man!*

THE DAILY SACRIFICES: ANOTHER PICTURE

We also see grain and wine in connection with the daily sacrifices. Burnt offerings were sacrificed day and night. Accompanying the burnt offering was a grain and a drink offering. It often goes unnoticed, but we can see here that bread and wine were offered along with the burnt offering.

"Now this is what you shall offer on the altar: two one year old lambs each day, continuously. The one lamb you shall offer in the morning and the other lamb you shall offer at twilight; and there shall be one-tenth of an ephah of fine flour mixed with one-fourth of a hin of beaten oil, and one-fourth of a hin of wine for a drink offering with one lamb. The other lamb you shall offer at twilight and shall offer with it the same grain offering and the same drink offering as in the morning, for a soothing aroma, an offering by fire to the Lord."

A "hin" of wine was approximately a gallon and a half, or about twenty-two liters. A quarter of a hin (5.5 liters) is about the same amount of blood an adult man would have in his body. What an appropriate picture we find in the Scriptures portraying Jesus's blood poured out for us!

Christ is the reality of the burnt offering. His life was wholly and totally consumed, continually offered to God, night and day, as a sweet-smelling aroma to God. The grain and the drink offerings (bread and wine) accompanying the burnt offering were reminders that the life Christ lived and the price he paid could not be separated from the blessings of the New Covenant which he secured for his beloved bride.

Under the law, drink offerings were not to be offered alone but in connection with the offerings of "soothing aroma" to the Lord, namely the burnt, meal, and peace offerings. They were never to be offered with the sin or trespass offerings. There was something about the drink offering of wine in the Old Testament that brought joy to God. There was joy for God in the burnt offering (Christ's life of total obedience), his sinless life (the meal offering), and his being our peace and reconciliation to God (the peace offering). But there was no joy for God in Christ's suffering when he became sin upon the cross (sin offering) and was the recipient of the wrath of God for each and every one of our sins (the trespass offering). This explains the absence of any drink offering accompanying the sin and trespass offerings.

THE PASSOVER CELEBRATION AND THE FEAST OF UNLEAVENED BREAD

Many people use the picture of the Passover celebration as a foreshadowing of the Lord's Supper. Lamb, unleavened bread, bitter herbs, and wine are prominent in that celebration. But interestingly, in the account of the Passover and Feast of Unleavened Bread recorded in Exodus 12, three of these elements were mentioned—but not the fourth. Wine is not mentioned. History tells us that wine only became part of the Passover celebration sometime following the captives' return from Babylon. But it is never mentioned in the Old Testament as part of the Passover celebration.

Why is this? Could it be that the symbols of the New Covenant—the bread *and the wine*—were only fully realized after the finished work of Christ on the cross, when the New

Covenant was initiated and the Old Covenant was made obsolete?

SUMMARY OF CHRIST IN THE OLD TESTAMENT PICTURES

It is Christ who is:

- Our high priest after the order of Melchizedek
- The I Am, who existed in eternity long before Abraham or the Levitical priesthood ever came into existence
- The reality of the Old Testament tabernacle (and temple) and the bread and wine contained therein
- The reality of the Old Testament sacrifices that were accompanied by the symbols of the New Covenant (bread and wine)

PRACTICAL APPLICATIONS FOR CELEBRATING THE LORD'S SUPPER

For the early Christians, the Lord's Supper was part of a festive meal. The first "Lord's Supper" was a full meal the Lord ate together with his disciples (actually a Passover Feast). It was *not* the "Lord's appetizer" or the "Lord's snack" consisting of a small, thin wafer and a thimbleful of wine or grape juice. It was a "supper," a banquet, or a festive meal, and in the early church it was known as an "agape feast." It was equivalent to what we would call a potluck today.

"While they were eating, he took some bread and after a blessing he broke it and gave it to them, and said, 'Take it, this is my body.' And when he had taken a cup and given thanks, he gave it to them,

and they all drank from it. And he said to them, 'This is my blood of the covenant, which is poured out for many.'" (Mark 14:22-24)

Twenty years later, when the church in Corinth was coming together to celebrate the Lord's Supper, they were taking a meal together.

"So then, my brothers and sisters, when you come together *to eat . . .*" (I Corinthians 11:33)

Though the Lord's Supper was celebrated as a full meal, the focal element or showcase of that meal was "the cup and the bread."

"Is not the cup of blessing which we bless a sharing in the blood of Christ? Is not the bread which we break a sharing in the body of Christ? Since there is one bread, we who are many are one body; for we all partake of the one bread." (1 Corinthians 10:16-17)

Dining with others, as they did in the book of Acts where they broke bread together, was associated with fellowship, gladness of heart, and praising God.

"They were continually devoting themselves to the apostles' teaching and to fellowship, to the breaking of bread and to prayer." (Acts 2:42)

"Day by day continuing with one mind in the temple, and breaking bread from house to house, they were taking their meals together with gladness and sincerity of heart, praising God and having favor with all the people. And the Lord was adding to their number day by day those who were being saved." (Acts 2:46-47)

By way of contrast, what is the basic mood or atmosphere in

most churches today when the Lord's Supper is taken? Is it one of celebration, joy, and gladness of heart—such as the atmosphere at a wedding? Or could it be better described as the atmosphere one would expect at a funeral—silence, sobriety, introspection, and seriousness?

The Lord's Supper was celebrated in homes, not in cathedrals; in smaller, dinner-sized groups, not in large formal gatherings.

"Day by day continuing with one mind in the temple, and breaking bread from house to house."

DO THIS IN REMEMBRANCE OF ME

When we partake of the Lord's Supper, we remember the Lord of the New Covenant together.

"I will put my law within them and on their heart I will write it."

When we gather for the Lord's Supper, we remember the things the Lord has done *in us* that we were unable to do ourselves. For example, when the Lord enables us to forgive someone who has offended us, when we were unable to forgive them ourselves, that's Lord's Supper material to bring to the meal and share with others!

"I will be their God, and they shall be my people."

When we gather for the Lord's Supper, we remember how he has been our God. For example, we remember his leading (he is our shepherd, our guide). When the Lord puts someone in our path with whom we end up sharing the gospel, that's Lord's Supper material to bring to the meal and share with others!

We can share about his deliverance (he is our deliverer). For example, when the Lord delivers us from some sin or some harmful circumstance, heals us, enlightens our minds to see where we may have been living in darkness, and then enables us to live in the light, that's Lord's Supper material to bring to the meal and share with others!

We can share about his feeding (he is our spiritual food and spiritual drink). For example, when he shows us something in the Word that strengthens us or puts a song in our hearts to encourage us, that is spiritual food and spiritual drink; that's Lord's Supper material to bring to the meal and share with others!

We can share about his peace (he is our peace; he is our rest). For example, when we have a difficult decision to make, and after we pray about it the Lord gives us peace and we know the direction we must go, that's Lord's Supper material to bring to the meal and share with others!

The same thing is true of knowing his victory (he is our victory), his goodness (he is our goodness), his mercy and grace (he is mercy and grace), his love (he is love), his life (he is our life), his wisdom (he is wisdom), the fellowship we have with other believers (he is our fellowship), and the benefits of being in his house (he is the source of all spiritual blessings). Knowing him in all of these ways (and more), that's Lord's Supper material to bring to the meal and share with others!

"I will forgive their iniquity, and their sin I will remember no more."

When we gather for the Lord's Supper, we also remember his forgiveness. He has forgiven us for all of our sins—past, present, and future. God poured out all of his wrath for sin on his Son. His wrath is totally satisfied. There is not one drop left to pour out on us. Our sins and lawless deeds he remembers no more. When he sees us, he sees us in Christ as righteous, totally forgiven, holy, blameless, without spot or wrinkle, and beautiful. Thankfulness for his forgiveness and for his love, for his dying on the cross for us, that's Lord's Supper material that we can bring to the meal and share with others!

THE LORD'S SUPPER: THE LOVE FEAST

Referred to in 1 Corinthians 11:33 and Jude 12, the Lord's Supper was known as a love feast. It was a meal at which believers from every ethnicity, background, and social and economic status came together to share a common meal, demonstrate their oneness in Christ, and remember the Lord. It was a time to re-member or re-constitute the body of Christ under its spiritual head and king, the Lord Jesus. The physical feast was meant to be a picture of the spiritual feast that is ours to enjoy in the person of the Lord Jesus. It is a time for *all* to share and partake of physical food and for *all* to share with one another the spiritual food (Christ) by which we all have been nourished, for mutual benefit and encouragement.

PROBLEMS CONCERNING THE PRACTICE OF THE LORD'S SUPPER IN THE NEW TESTAMENT: 1 CORINTHIANS 11:17–34

"But in giving this instruction, I do not praise you, because you come together not for the better but for the worse."

Eating in an Unworthy Manner:

First Corinthians 11:27 presents a difficult passage for many Christians: "Therefore whoever eats the bread or drinks the cup of the Lord in an unworthy manner, shall be guilty of the body and the blood of the Lord."

When we look at the context of this verse, we find that a problem had developed in the way the Corinthian believers were taking the Lord's Supper. There were a few in the church who were wealthy and who brought food and wine to the banquet, and others who were not so wealthy who brought what they could. Then there were the slaves and the unemployed, who could bring nothing. The slaves, who often had to work late, would finally arrive to find that all the food had been eaten and all the wine had been drunk.

The picture that they were all one in Christ and all had become partakers of the same spiritual food had broken down. Some of the early guests could not control themselves and wait for the others. They were gluttons. They ate all the food, leaving nothing for latecomers. They drank more than their portion of wine, and some got drunk, some got sick, and others passed out ("fell asleep").

Eating in an Unworthy Manner Resulting in Judgment:

"But a person must examine himself, and in so doing he is to eat of the bread and drink of the cup. For he who eats and drinks, eats and drinks judgment to himself if he does not judge the body rightly."

The judgment here is judgment from the body, not judgment resulting in loss of salvation.

"So then, my brothers and sisters, when you come together to eat, wait for one another. If anyone is hungry, let him eat at home so that you will not come together for judgment."

In Roman society, the rich didn't like eating with the poor. The wealthier Christians in Corinth were judging the poor with evil motives. They did not see them as equal members in the body of Christ, so they did not wait for them.

When people came in late and all the food was gone and people were drunk, the latecomers judged those who had not waited for them as being selfish and indulgent, gluttons and drunkards. This, too, brought disunity in the body. This was not what the Lord's Supper was intended to represent. It was intended to portray a corporate sharing and partaking of the life of the Lord, not every person for himself.

Examining Yourselves:

"But a person must examine himself, and in so doing he is to eat of the bread and drink of the cup."

Examining oneself does not mean to become pious and introspective, trying to think of every sin you might have ever committed and confessing it so as to become worthy to partake of the Lord's Supper. We could *never* become worthy by anything we do. But Christ has *made* us worthy by his death on the cross, once for all.

"Examine yourself" was an admonition to make sure that the believers in Corinth were thinking of others and not taking more than their share of food or drink so as to incur judgment by the rest of the body, resulting in impaired relationships, broken fellowship, and disunity in the body of Christ. Many places today where only a small thimble-full of wine and a small wafer are offered as the substance for the Lord's Supper, this admonition would not even apply!

The way the Lord's Supper is practiced today has become perverted. The common belief that people must examine themselves, reflect upon their sins, and confess every possible sin before they partake of the Lord's Supper in order to avoid judgment and damnation creates an atmosphere of fear and gloom which negates Christ's finished work on the cross.

Is there "now no condemnation for those who are in Christ Jesus," or if we fail to confess every single sin and partake of the Lord's Supper in an "unworthy manner" will we be incurring his wrath and condemnation? Which is it?

Earlier in 1 Corinthians, Paul wrote to them that:

- They had been sanctified
- They were saints (holy ones)
- They were not lacking in any gift
- Christ would confirm them to the end, blameless
- They were in Christ, who became to them wisdom from God, righteousness, sanctification, and redemption

- They were a temple of God, and the Spirit of God dwelt in them
- The temple of God is holy (which they were)
- They were filled, rich, kings
- They were washed, sanctified, and justified
- They were joined (married) to the Lord, and were one spirit with him

In Corinth, the problem was a case of rich/poor prejudice. In some places, there may be prejudice based on skin color, ethnicity, nationality, or place in the cultural caste system. Regardless, these kinds of divisions are wrong. If we have impaired relationships with our brothers and sisters, we are to seek reconciliation so that we can truly celebrate our unity in Christ, just as our Lord taught, "Therefore if you are presenting your offering at the altar, and there remember that your brother has something against you, leave your offering there before the altar and go first be reconciled to your brother, and then come and present your offering." (Matthew 5:24)

Some may protest and say that there is grave danger of judgment from the Lord if we take the Lord's Supper in an "unworthy manner." I would respond by saying, yes, if people persist in disregarding the Lord's voice, ignoring his warnings, and hardening their hearts toward him and members of his body, we should expect that he will exercise some form of discipline or judgment. But it would be a redemptive judgment with a view of restoration—not of eternal damnation.

The cup that we drink is, indeed, the cup of the New Covenant, in which we can celebrate that our sins and lawless deeds he will remember no more (see Hebrews 10:7)! Therefore, we can approach the Lord's Supper with an attitude of celebration, not of fear.

The cup we drink as we celebrate the Lord's Supper is to be a Cup of Joy!

FREEDOM TO CELEBRATE

The celebration of the Lord's Supper as a communal Christian banquet in the first century was *never* a sacred ritual performed by a sacred person in a sacred building. Nowhere in the New Testament does it say that the Lord's Supper must be administered by a pastor, a clergyman, or a priest or conducted inside a building with a cross on top of it. And where on earth did we ever get the notion that the bread and the wine, taken as a meal along with other believers in someone's home, is out of date and has been superseded by a superior model of partaking of a small, tasteless wafer and a thimble-sized portion of grape juice while sitting on a hard bench in a warehouse-sized room full of people, most of whom you don't know?

The message of the Lord's Supper is revolutionary! It was as revolutionary then as it is today.

It is interesting to note that three primary questions fueled the fires of a revolution in the 1960s in America known as the Jesus Movement. Young people were questioning America's involvement in the Vietnam War, "hippies" were dropping out of society and displaying their distinctions by growing their hair long, wearing "holey jeans" and flowers in their hair, and smoking pot. Traditional morality and marriage were being questioned. Traditional values were being questioned, like the necessity for completing college and getting a "good job."

Within the church, too, people started to question. This was an era when many people—especially young people—dropped out of the traditional church because they didn't find it relevant. They just couldn't relate. This resulted in number of alternatives for traditional church being born, such as Christian communes, coffeehouses, and numerous parachurch organizations. As was the chant in secular society, so became the chant within the organized church: "Power to the people!"

Within both evangelical and charismatic circles, Christian leaders whom the majority of young people in that generation were looking to were focusing on three main questions:

1. Where in the New Testament does it say that you have to be an ordained pastor, clergyman, or priest with a seminary education, in order to preside over the Lord's Supper?
2. Where in the New Testament does it say that you have to be an ordained pastor, clergyman, or priest with a seminary education, in order to baptize someone?
3. And where does it say that this has to happen inside a church building?

This resulted in groups of college students and "lay people" from across the nation gathering together on beaches, at rivers, lakes, and swimming pools to publicly worship and baptize new believers into the body of Christ. It was also a time when people began to seek a more biblical, first-century experience of the Lord's Supper, away from the formal confines of church buildings, and back in homes where the practice originated. It was a time of revival and a moving of the Holy Spirit. And it was characterized by a great outpouring of joy and a sense of freedom.

SUMMARY

"Therefore let us celebrate the feast . . . with the unleavened bread of sincerity and truth." (1 Corinthians 5:8)

The Lord's Supper Is a Celebration of Our Oneness with Christ
"The sons of this age marry and are given in marriage, but those who are considered worthy to attain to that age and the resurrection from the dead, neither marry nor are given in marriage." (Luke 20:34-35)

We are the bride of Christ! The reason there will be no marriage in the age to come is because we will be married to Christ! This is true whether we've realized it or not. When we said "yes" and accepted him as our Lord and Savior, that relationship began! He is our Bridegroom. We will be one with him to enjoy him, to be to him a life companion, and to rule and reign with him for all eternity.

THE MYSTERIES OF GOD

The New Testament is filled with mysteries! Mark wrote of

the mystery of the kingdom. John wrote of the mystery of the seven stars and the seven golden lampstands and the mystery of Babylon the Great in the book of Revelation. But it is Paul's writings most of all that are full of mysteries.

Paul wrote of:

- The mystery of the partial hardening of Israel until the fullness of the Gentiles has come
- The mystery of the resurrection
- The mystery of God's will—the summing up of all things in Christ
- The mystery hidden from the ages that the Gentiles were fellow heirs with the Jews, of the same body, and partakers of the same promises in Christ
- The mystery that through the church the manifold wisdom of God would be made known to the principalities and powers in heavenly places according to God's eternal purpose
- The mystery of the gospel
- The mystery of Christ in you, the hope of glory
- The mystery of lawlessness
- The mystery of the faith
- The mystery of godliness

The Mega-Mystery

But there is one other mystery that Paul wrote about. He called it the "great mystery," or in the Greek, the *mega*-mystery.

It was the granddaddy of all mysteries, the whopper! This also is revealed in the letter to the Ephesians.

Think about how we use the word *mega* today. The mega-rich—people who are not just rich, but fabulously rich. Mega-churches—not just small churches, but churches with membership in the thousands.

Paul wrote of many mysteries, but this mystery, he calls the mega-mystery!

What is this mystery? It is the mystery that the husband-wife relationship is a picture to us that we are the bride of Christ—the wife of the Lamb!

In the passage where Paul wrote of the marriage relationship between man and woman and husbands loving their wives as Christ loved the church and gave himself for her, he concluded with a quote from Genesis and then identified the mystery of all mysteries.

"For this reason a man shall leave his father and mother and be joined to his wife, and the two shall become one flesh."

Then he dropped the bomb: "This mystery is great [Greek: *mega*] but I am speaking with reference to Christ and the church." (Ephesians 5:31-32)

This mega-mystery was foretold in the Old Testament:

"'And it will come about in that day,' declares the Lord, 'That you will call me Ishi [my husband] and will no longer call me Baali [my master, or my Baal] . . . I will betroth you to me forever; Yes, I will betroth you to me in righteousness and in justice.'" (Hosea 2:16, 19)

THIS MEGA-MYSTERY IS THAT TO THE LORD ALONE
WE HAVE BEEN ETERNALLY BONDED IN A ONENESS FAR
GREATER THAN THE EARTHLY PICTURE OF MARRIAGE
COULD BUT FAINTLY PORTRAY. THIS IS THE MYSTERY WE
CELEBRATE EVERY TIME WE TAKE THE LORD'S SUPPER!

BIBLIOGRAPHY

Amaral, Joe, *Understanding Jesus,* New York, NY: Faith Words, a division of Hachette Book Group, Inc., 2011.

Davidson, Mark, *Becoming the Beloved,* White Oaks, TX: Shulamite Ministries Publishing, 2010.

George, Bob, *Baptism and the Lord's Supper, a Visual Aid to Spiritual Truth,* [Audio Cassettes], Dallas, TX: People to People.

Witherington III, Ben, *Making a Meal of It,* Waco, TX; Baylor University Press, 2007.

SCRIPTURE INDEX

OTHER BOOKS FROM THIS AUTHOR ARE
AVALIABLE THROUGH
Benchpress Publishing
P.O. Box 5846
Charlottesville, VA 22905
www.BobEmeryBooks.com

THE NEW COVENANT
The Dramatic Story Behind the Faith Once For All Delivered to the Saints

In *The New Covanent*, you will see how this covenant was progressively realized and played out in the captivating saga of the first-century church as God himself embroidered the extraordinary message into the lives of his people, specifically through the eyes of the apostle John.

HIS DESIRE IS FOR ME
A 30-Day Devotional and Commentary on the Song of Songs

Blending fiction, commentary, and 30-days of devotions, *His Desire Is for Me* provides daily, bite-sized portions of the Song of Songs for you to savor, meditate upon, and enjoy. It reveals the different stages believe go through on the road to spiritual maturity in their love for the Lord, from an initial love, to an increasing love, and finally unfolding into a mature love. Read it, and you will come to believe, with conviction, that His desire is truly for you!

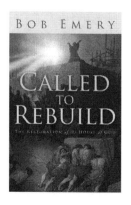

CALLED TO REBUILD
The Restoration of the House of God

A commentary on Ezra and Nehemiah, along with the other "remnant books" of the Old Testament – Haggai, Zechariah, and Malachi. *Called to Rebuild* examines these precious books and draws application for those who would be the spiritual descendants of that remnant in this generation. This book is for those who have a heart to rebuild and see the church become all that God intended for it to be.

Made in the USA
Coppell, TX
01 May 2021

54723255R00026